Little Pebble™

Habitats

All About
Wetlands

by Christina Mia Gardeski

raintree 🍃

a Capstone company — publishers for children

Raintree is an imprint of Capstone Global Library Limited, a company incorporated in England and Wales having its registered office at 264 Banbury Road, Oxford, OX2 7DY – Registered company number: 6695582

www.raintree.co.uk
myorders@raintree.co.uk

Edited by Marissa Kirkman
Designed by Juliette Peters (cover) and Charmaine Whitman (interior)
Picture research by Eric Gohl
Production by Katy LaVigne
Originated by Capstone Global Library Limited
Printed and bound in India.

ISBN 978 1 4747 5267 1
21 20 19 18 17
10 9 8 7 6 5 4 3 2 1

British Library Cataloguing in Publication Data
A full catalogue record for this book is available from the British Library.

Acknowledgements
We would like to thank the following for permission to reproduce photographs: Getty Images: Doxieone Photography, 17; iStockphoto: maimai, 20; Shutterstock: AlxYago, 9, baxys, 21, Dj7, 11, HelloRF Zcool, 5, lafoto, 7, lazyllama, 15, Melok, back cover, interior (reeds illustration), Michael G McKinne, 19, N_Belonogov, cover, Romrodphoto, 1, sahua d, 16, skynetphoto, 13

Every effort has been made to contact copyright holders of material reproduced in this book. Any omissions will be rectified in subsequent printings if notice is given to the publisher.

All the Internet addresses (URLs) given in this book were valid at the time of going to press. However, due to the dynamic nature of the Internet, some addresses may have changed, or sites may have changed or ceased to exist since publication. While the author and publisher regret any inconvenience this may cause readers, no responsibility for any such changes can be accepted by either the author or the publisher.

Contents

What is a wetland?

A wetland is a low land.

It is filled with water.

Rain falls.

Tides flow in.

A wetland holds the water.

This stops floods.

8

Marsh

Grass grows in a marsh.

The water can be shallow.

11

A marsh is a wet habitat.

Crabs lay eggs here.

Fish hide.

crab

Swamp

Trees grow in a swamp.

The water can be deep.

The tree trunks are thick.

Ducks nest here.

Alligators swim.

Bog

Moss grows in a bog.

The land is soft and wet.

moss

Plants rot in a bog.

Insects eat the plants.

Frogs eat the insects.

frog

Glossary

bog wetland with wet and soft ground where moss grows

flood water that overflows onto dry land

habitat home of a plant or animal

marsh shallow wetland where grass grows

moss small, low plants without flowers that grow in bogs

shallow not deep

swamp deep wetland where trees grow

tide flow of water in and out in an ocean or river

trunk centre stem of a tree from bottom to top, separate from its branches

Read more

Marshes and Pools (Horrible Habitats), Sharon Katz Cooper (Raintree, 2010)

Rock Pool Animals (Animals in Their Habitats), Sian Smith (Raintree, 2015)

Wetlands (Habitat Survival), Buffy Silverman (Raintree, 2013)

Websites

www.bbc.co.uk/education/topics/zx882hv
Discover more about habitats and the environment.

www.dkfindout.com/uk/animals-and-nature/
habitats-and-ecosystems/wetlands/
Find out more about wetlands.

Index